I Swallow Turquoise for Courage

Volume 61

Sun Tracks

An American Indian Literary Series

Series Editor

Ofelia Zepeda

Editorial Committee

Larry Evers

Joy Harjo

Geary Hobson

N. Scott Momaday

Irvin Morris

Simon J. Ortiz

Emory Sckaquaptewa

Kate Shanley

Leslie Marmon Silko

Luci Tapahonso

I Swallow Turquoise for Courage

Poems by Hershman R. John

The University of Arizona Press   Tucson

The University of Arizona Press
© 2007 Hershman R. John

Library of Congress Cataloging-in-Publication Data
John, Hershman R., 1972–
  I swallow turquoise for courage : poems / by Hershman
R. John.
      p. cm. — (Sun tracks : an American Indian literary
series ; v. 61)
    ISBN 978-0-8165-2592-8 (pbk. : acid-free paper)
    1. Indians of North America—Poetry. I. Title.
PS3610.O257I17 2007
811'.6—dc22   2007005312

Publication of this book is made possible in part by
the proceeds of a permanent endowment created with
the assistance of a Challenge Grant from the National
Endowment for the Humanities, a federal agency.

Manufactured in the United States of America on acid-free,
archival-quality paper.

12 11 10 09   6 5 4 3 2

For my mother, Marjorie

For my father, Russell

For my sister, Avarae

For my grandmothers:
Susie Worker and Mary John

For Coyote

For James

Contents

4. Theory of Light

 **Two Bodies of Elements**

Two Bodies of Elements

1.

Lake, Billy Ann, Carmen and me
Went to Luther Burbank Elementary together,
Lived in the same apartment complex,
Did homework, and created games.
We played "King, Castle and Maidens."
One day the maidens became bored with playing
In my Kingdom. My subjects don't listen well.
We went to Carmen's place. Two doors down
To play a new game in her family's
Backroom, a dungeon with green shag carpet.

On a long brown leather couch slept Michael,
Carmen's older brother. *He was Thor slumbering.*
Thor after a battle with ice giants . . . .
He covered the couch like a large homemade star
Quilt. No shirt on, his skin a still lake.
Lying on his belly, his long blonde hair
Flowed over the couch. A bulky body
Heavy as sand. A sun-tanned back
Hooked to a sloping rock shoulder, arm then hand.
His red shorts were too small for his legs—
Thick ice blocks the length of the couch.
Face hidden, he breathed out deeply
Like a horse or the north wind.
> *I thought everything*
> *On him looked awkward, like a big scaly fish*
> *With tiny eyes.*
He was tired from high school teachers,
Varsity football practice, homework.

Slowly my fascination built. I'd never
Seen a man before.

A frying pan, a fork and butter knife—
Carmen brought them to the couch
By the resting boulder. Quietly,
She prepared water with paper towels in a bowl,
As a nurse would alcohol and cotton swabs.
      "We have to cut out his heart, because
      He doesn't need it."
It reminded me of sheep
Who became roasted mutton at Grandma's
In Sand Springs. She sharpened her
Knife on a smooth stone. Then placed
A plastic bowl under the sheep's neck.
Cut tenderly.

Lake and Billy Ann snickered at her joke.
      I was stunned, like I had fallen
            Off monkey bars.
            Lost my breath . . . .
     "Turn the patient over," Carmen ordered me.
     I flushed red. *What if he woke up?*
         He was a giant.
His back thick ham slabs, too heavy.
His throwing arm a yellow surfboard.
His legs concrete posts holding up the pier,
Too big to handle. *I could never turn him.*
      "Don't be afraid," she snapped.
I walked to his side, touched his smooth back,
A hot, hot stove. His back moved hard
Reacting like a car engine, a tiger.

I imagined him turning,
Eyes—deep blue. He'd have a thick chest,
My chest when I turn 20.
We'd have similar bodies.

2.

Toward the sand dunes by the empty black house,
Blue sky, tan sand, green yucca and lavender
Earth, a lizard sat under the yucca shading
Himself from the heat. The sand was too hot to play on.
Grandma washed her hair with yucca root,
Sudsy and wet. She combed her hair with an old
Plastic brush. She wore just a red velvet skirt,
Nothing else. I could smell her pot of mutton stew
Boiling over with colored corn and squash. She knew how
To feed her young. She was as giving as the soil or sand.
        Her skin was golden brown like her own
Frybread, her arm thick piñon tree branches—weathered,
Unbreakable. Her breasts were crested sand dunes
Without the yucca, cracked clay or lizards.
Her breasts were the shifting sand, wind-swept,
The way a sidewinder glides across the warmth. Her aureoles
The San Francisco peaks in the distance. Her prayers
The yellowing corn stalks in the breeze.
        Nothing as pure. Looking back,
I still see Grandma washing her hair. Water dripping
Off her nipples and soft belly, streaming into mud.
Her red skirt big as a parachute all around her, damp
And alive. She shakes out her hair like a cat does.
Sprinkles moisten my skin. Her skillful weaving hands
Take each strand of hair and begin to weave,
Tying hair into a tsiiyéél, a hair-knot.

Yesterday, the rain fell on her black house.
She likes the wet sand mixing with dancing rain—cool liquid
Fingers over her hair, her body. Strands of rain fell like dew
Sliding off spider webs, long and speckled, sweeping stories.
When a cool drop hit her brown hand, it soothed
Her skin. Her hands as strong as lightning
Snaking from the sky to lap the earth.
      Boom! Thunder!
      She smiles.
      Each drop stretches from cloud to earth.
Her strands of jet-black hair are everywhere
Touching rain, filling our washes with sand-red water
For her horses, sheep, fevered lizards.
She still smiles, the deepness in her face
Our red canyons spreading across nihikéyah,
Lifting up our land to the south of our fields
Of corn, squash and melons to keep the Hunger People
And the ghost of Kit Carson's lost cavalry away.
Her smile shows white teeth cutting into the Grand Canyon.
Her voice cries in the eagle's wing, the horse's gallop, cracking
Fire, whirlwind over leaves, frogs near a mud pond.
Her fingernail is the new moon tonight, another is the white
Owl. Her green army jacket hangs over the chair.
Her scarves float through the air as bluejays, cardinals, doves . . . .
Her hands rub my aching leg, her breath warming the bone.
Her footsteps track across the night from star to sleeping
      Grandchild. I love watching sunsets,
Remembering the yucca root suds in her hair,
Water moistening red earth into mud again. I love
Smelling Grandma's sweet hair bringing the rain home.

Coyote's Eyes

for Roddy Yellowman

Location: Green Beach
Western Australia, October 1991
Mission: Combat War Games

My brother Roddy blended into the shrubs and sand.
        His pupils were like charcoal.
The moon reflected off the black sea.
        The moon was his grandmother watching.
The humid air closed around him, his M-16.
        He was quiet, breathing in, hold a breath.
It was a rule of the Marines:
        "Your rifle is an extension of your body."
He crawled on his belly like a coyote
        Ready to pounce on a sleeping jackrabbit.

Coyote called out to his brothers,
        "Brothers, come help push my rock."
He wanted to play with the lizards—
        They were sliding down the hill on smooth stones.
All the little desert lizards ran up the hill
        Pushing the great rock with tiny arms.
The elder lizard stood at the bottom
        Shaking his head in disapproval.
The rock groaned and cracked.
        Coyote smiled as pebbles rolled down.

Roddy crawled up the hill to the west.
        He was scout for the military game.
With his night-vision goggles, he scanned for the Aussies
        But saw no movement, no fires, nothing.

The vision through the goggles reminded him of Navajoland.

       IIe was home, except the sound of the surf was wrong.

His radio crackled as he turned it on.

       "Sir, everything's dead," he whispered.

He hid next to a great shrub.

       "Yeah, Yellowman, keep your eyes open," said Sergeant Vega.

Then Roddy heard pebbles rolling down the hill.

       It wasn't him . . . .

The rock gave way with a great thundering crack.

       Coyote went underneath it, rolling down the hill.

"There's someone out here!" yelled Roddy into the radio

       As the sound of crackling leaves came through the shrubs.

The shrub exploded, a bomb made of leaves and twigs.

       Keep your eyes open, keep eyes . . .

Overhead, a great force of wind knocked him over

       And he rolled down the hill . . . .

With eyes huge as trouts', they watched in awe.

       All the desert lizards saw the rolling fall.

They scrambled for safety out of his path

       And stood watching to see what would happen

Next, as the dancing dust settled.

At the bottom of the hill, they could see nothing—

       Darkness . . . . They were both blind.

Coyote's beautiful blue eyes popped out of his head

       And rolled into a stream, lost.

Roddy's binoculars fell from his brown hand

       And rolled into night's blanket, gone.

"Ayáh! Ayáh!" cried Roddy and Coyote from the pain.

       "Ch'íídii ni'," they cursed.

Coyote tried to get up,
>
> But the rock tore his body apart.

One arm went to the East,
>
> The other to the West.

One leg went to the North
>
> And the other to the South.

Roddy tried to get up,
>
> But his back was hurting,

"Your rifle is an extension of your body."
>
> His rifle was gone to the directions.

He'd lost his protective arms.

All the lizards laughed
>
> Until tears came to their eyes.

Two crows fell from the hands of Grandfather Sky.
>
> They were trying to breathe, laugh, and fly.

It was funny to see Coyote fall apart.

On the hilltop, the radio called his name:
>
> "Corporal Yellowman! Yellowman! Yellowman!"

He climbed his way back up the hill—
>
> "Uh . . . Sir . . ." Roddy slowly breathed into the radio.

"What happened, Yellowman?" Sarge Vega replied.
>
> "I don't know?"   "You don't know!"

"The bush next to me exploded and knocked me down . . ."
>
> "A bush? . . ." "It was a God-damn roo!" "A roo?"

"A roo . . . . A kangaroo. Didn't you ever see one?"
>
> Roddy started to laugh until he couldn't breathe.

Vega heard an echo of laughter in the distance.
>
> It reminded him of coyotes yapping at the moon.

"Come help me, my little brothers," howled Coyote.

He had no eyes, arms, or legs.

"I told you not to play with us," instructed the elder lizard.

He stood looking at the log Coyote had become.

"Help me, brother."   "Dooda!"   "Why, brother?"

"Only if you never play with us again."

"I will never play with you again."

Roddy found his rifle as the first rays of the sun

Peeked over the blue-black ocean dawn.

The elder lizard instructed the little lizards.

They ran to the four directions and brought back Coyote's limbs.

They put his arms and legs crookedly back on.

Finally Coyote stood and said, "I can't see."

His eyes were lost in the stream.

So the elder lizard whispered to the two crows.

They flew to a nearby hogan over the hill.

At a firepit, the two crows picked up charcoal bits.

The elder lizard told Coyote to look up to the sky.

He looked up and saw nothing.

The crows dropped their hot coals

Into Coyote's eye sockets, and he screamed.

Everyone saw Coyote running in circles,

And they all began to laugh, again.

Roddy found his night-vision goggles behind a bush.

As he stood up to stretch,

He blinked his tired charcoal eyes.

He wondered if the youthfulness would ever return.

He watched the moon begin to set into the Australian Ocean.

In the fading whiteness
He saw the face of his grandmother, going home
      She spoke in broken English, finishing her Coyote story:
"That's why when you see a coyote,
      His body is twisted, raggedy.
His eyes, black and empty.
      No longer pretty."

A Sheep Dog Locked in Photograph

All the old photographs, hidden like buried
Treasure. Broken prayer sticks under my dreams

And my worn mattress. Each one like a postcard sent back
Home; wonders only seen in slick travel magazines.

Boxed up under my bed, colored souls on Kodak paper—
I can still see Grandma's smile next to her resting sheep dog.

Like a blue lightning strike over the northern sky,
Over two black houses, I pull the first leaf out, at random.

A picture-flash: Tom and Susie Worker are sitting together
On a couch covered with a large Navajo Chief's blanket woven

By her brown hands and sheep's wool. The pattern of stripes—
Blue to black to white, shifting like rain clouds to clear skies.

My grandparents look tired. The day was Christmas 1992,
With a little bit of snow on the Earth. Tired from traveling

Over 100 miles away from their painted desert
To the city, tired from raising eleven children of the Deer

Spring before the Depression, before Roosevelt,
Before the World Wars, before computers, before

Satellite phones and televisions . . . . Outside, the north wind
Was blowing Tuba City away. But, Grandma's and Grandpa's

Eyes are glazed red from happiness. Outside,
The clouds swelled full of snow and ice.

A blue lightning flash, another photograph, another place:
New York, 1985: I see the Statue of Liberty, tiny, like a pin

Stuck in the gray ocean, surrounded by the wrought metal
Edges of Gotham City. It was the only picture I took:

The dollar-bill green lady holding her torch, guiding
Moths, reality, men and ferries. As she stood in iconic

Pose, Grandma flooded back, quickly: strong in her own green
Velvet dress, she stretched dough over her palms, making frybread.

A foghorn wailed just past the Emerald City's fiery torch.
My mind refocused on the warm glow of a new moon.

The Lady's light filled the starless sky like Grandma's teardrop
Turquoise and silver brooch. Made from a thousand tiny Kingman

Nuggets, its shine captured in a perfect burst—
A sunflower high on a green stem. Each seed a raindrop

Made of smooth sky. When the sun touched the brooch,
It was blinding. A perfect mosaic of water-light-sky stones.

A blue strike—bright from a cigarette—steals Lady Liberty's light.
The Staten Island ferry moves on to Crow Agency, Montana.

At Custer Battlefield, my cousins smile for a picture, tourists
Next to Custer's grave. Defiant, wearing dark shades,

They hold up cans of Coors Light waiting for Custer to rise
Again so they can take up their bows, arrows, uzis. Warriors,

Proud and ready to hide deep in the yellowtail prairie grass.
Their women and children safe in tipi camps by the Little

Bighorn River. I know they would die again and again. Rise
Again and again to put up more white marble tombstones.

They would do this to save our future children, to save our
Grandmas—Mary Black Eagle, Susie Worker, Great Great Great

Grandmother Lefthand . . . . They would save our grandfathers too—
Sonny Black Eagle, Tom Worker, the horned toad . . . .

Lodge Grass Indians, the high school basketball team, plays
A few miles from Mary's block house and her ten grazing horses.

Her basketball team is waiting for the final winning basket
To end time, an orange ball to shoot dead the visiting team

From Billings. Another war of *Savages versus Whites*.
Won this time by the "Skins"—Class "B" State Champs again.

Two Leggings, a '49, a warrior's party. The tranquil dark
Raven feathers, a deep cold night fueled by a bonfire and beer.

Victory runs hot, steaming piss into the trout-filled river
Lined by a hundred cars, nights caws, and some more tame

Drinking brawls. All night long, the happy Indian basketball
Warriors sing '49 songs: *We won, but my dark-hair girlfriend*

Left with one of the blue-eyed. He na ya na . . . .
My brothers smile with big white teeth, have strong backs like their

Broncos and are blessed with good looks. That's what Crow boys
Do best—look good and play good ball. I wish Grandma Susie

Was here to see her young Crow and Navajo boys, their hearts full
Of wild war ponies. But because of old age, she was put in a home

Where she is reverting back into a baby—quivering mouth, softening
Body like melting ice cream, wetting her bed—as her nurse-mother sighs.

Grandma is there captured within the state-certified white walls.
Reflections appear—Kit Carson, Custer, Andrew Jackson's ghosts—

In the many stainless steel items of the room: the nearby syringe,
The mirror, the drinking cup, the stethoscope. The nurse turns off

The television, it buzzes and flashes a bright blue dot that burns
In my grandmother's retina. More ghosts appear, this time as lost

Shadows on film behind the great family photo. Our pasts
Flood back from the Sea of Forgetfulness . . . . Old girlfriends,

Old boyfriends, old wives, old husbands—grainy moments belonging
To brothers, cousins, sisters, friends. Their demands are frenzied

As mean seagulls overwhelming me holding a bag of popcorn:
Burn those! Burn them up! Why the hell did you keep them alive?!

I should burn them so that the stars can smell the rising visions.
When the sunrise burns the nightmares, like flies stuck on the silk

In a dreamcatcher, the visions explode into flares. Bright as a blue
Ball lightning floating mysteriously over Grandma Susie's place.

Her reservation home with its sleek red canyons, rabbit brush,
Sand dunes, is like seeing Giza's pyramids, Disneyland, Stonehenge,

The Grand Canyon. A place filled with the awe of fairy dust,
A dinosaur's tooth, a pure gold coin. I pick up the last

Leaf that floats into my hands. Here, Grandma's sheep corral
Is empty of foul smells. And there staring at me is my last image:

A sheep dog locked in photograph. Grandma's sheep dogs
Never have names and the only word they ever learn

And know is "Dibé!" "Dibé!" "Dibé!"
A command as heavy as hail shattering a windshield:

"Dibé!" Go back to the sheep, now! Watch over them!
Watch out for sheep-stealing coyotes.

They all run like hurt boys glancing up to see if the sky will fall.
This one sheep dog is a mutt sitting next to his empty

Dog dish—a Chevy hubcap. His eyes are black marbles:
One eye is Hungry, one eye is Lonely. With only

A life span of three years, a sheep dog dies from the elements,
Fighting a mountain lion, or from a gunshot wound

(For developing a taste for tender lamb).
Taking care of sheep is their story. Like the many tribes

Wiped out from smallpox long before the white man
Gave the tribe a history, and because we forgot them,

They, the sheep dogs, die nameless too. When Grandma was happy
With her sheep dogs, she would feed them a can of government

Peanut butter and watch them chew, chew, chew. Licking.
She watched each one lick its teeth and fur for hours . . . .

I can still hear her laughing about her sheep dogs.

Wooden Duck

Just to think, I may be the first.
I walk through the small iron door,
       small like an Anasazi opening.
There on the stool
       a bearded English man pours sour ale.

The stained glass windows speak a story:
       a running rabbit, a human caterpillar,
       a disappearing cat, and a queen of hearts.
My emotions ebb like those of Alice's, out of place.

Outside the window—
       a green hill supporting Windsor castle.
It stands like an adobe village atop a mesa.
The ground is black soil,
No signs of the red reservation dirt.

A small black bird perches on the wooden sill.
Is it a corn-stealing reservation chicken?
No. It's a Scottish raven, an Indian crow mirage.

No frybread with mutton stew.
I order Yorkshire pudding,
A meat pie.

Around the pub
       spreads the spired city of learning: Oxford.
Like tipis of the annual Crow Fair,
       these colleges choke the town:

Pembroke, Old Crow; St. Peters, Black Eagle; Christ Church,
Red Wolf; Magdalen, Old Coyote . . . .

Here in the pub
        Queen Elizabeth rules by her crown.
Across the great diving lakes,
Within the sacred mountains,
Grandmother Little Owl weaves her loom.

In this room,
I am the red Columbus.
There are no other Indian brothers.

I hear the echo of an eagle,
The sun dance drums,
Whistling canyons.
But the wailing spirits of Stonehenge
        silence their chants.

I truly am the first Navajo in the Wooden Duck.

 **Post-Modernity in Kayenta**

Watering the Sheep

after Basho

An old frog
Jumps into the sky—
Splash!

Dark Navajo boy
Sitting under evergreens
Eating hard frybread.

A roadrunner, big
As a chicken strikes the pond—
Swallowing wet jade.

Sheep and goats nibble
Sweet grass at the water's edge.
The sheep dog laps blue.

The horned toad's eyes
Oblivious to the light
Wait for a buzzing.

The lightning bird skips
Over the toad, over the boy's
Foot, into the pines.

Heat waves hang above—
Even the tree's shade is hot.
His lips are sand dunes.

Another frog jumps.
The sheep move onto ripe reeds
Chewing and splashing.

Grandma kneads a cloud.
She lets it rise, heats a pan—
Bread waits for her sheep.

Post-Modernity in Kayenta

after Elizabeth Bishop

for Scott Manning Stevens

The monoliths, sandstone
carvings crest high
in the air, tall like redwoods
with striking wind-eroded,
rain-washed, sunny edges.
Driving from the East,
two lovers from Chicago
discover a new city
made of sand cliffs,
rabbit brush, red soil,
a prairie dog's echoes,
heavy dark clouds,
sharp yucca. Sheep dot
the valley, nibbling on
wild green shoots.
Monument Valley—
50 miles from Kayenta.
A small Navajo town
holding onto the edges
of the Earth, encircled
by purple mountains,
dry mud washes, jackrabbit
burrows, shifting sand slopes,
coyote tracks, some
small thirsty juniper trees . . .
Four cows walk slowly
away from the sun to
the nearest gas station

looking for shade.
On the AAA map,
the road breaks
into two black veins:
interstate or road?
K-town to San Diego.
With no trendy clubs nearby,
these two hungry men see the neon
hamburger sign: Burger King.
Like walking into a Life magazine
pictorial of the Southwest, the men
walk through the pages of the fast-
food chain. There are four Navajo
families, their grandmothers
wearing glossy crushed velvet
dresses colored with deep splashes
of late-spring orchids, red or purple.
Decorated like royalty with turquoise
and silver bracelets, intricate inlaid
pins and concho belts. Around
their weathered necks are long
strands of white shell, coral or heavy
silver squash blossoms. Their black
hair tied back with white yarn
in a tight figure-eight bun.
On the bright orange walls
are the large black and white photos—
The Navajo Code Talkers,
watching grandfathers dressed
in pollen-yellow uniforms
and apple-red military caps,
with metal stars and stripes
pinned to them. Their eyes

are pieces of charcoal
already burnt-out from seeing war
and sleeping among dead bodies.
Even the Blessing Way ceremonies
can't purify their cataracts.
During WWII, they talked in code,
in a language reserved
for the wind. Or bears.
A code the Japanese couldn't break:
the wind's whistle or the bear's growl—
drowning Asian intonations
and clicking grasshoppers.
These grandfathers
saved the country so their
screaming grandchildren
could learn to be Diné and run
around and around holding
half a hamburger and spilling
broken pieces of French fries across
ivory tiles. One little girl,
dark and pretty with high cheek-
bones and messy hair,
smiles at the attractive blond
man waiting to order.
Holding her hand up high
she shows him her kid's meal toy.
Lewis sees the plastic details:
a perfect smile, candy-apple red lips,
large breasts, dark eyes, purple eye
shadow, a buckskin dress,
long frozen black hair,
with a rock turquoise necklace.

It's one of the many Disney
Girls—Pocahontas. He smiles,
imagining this Navajo girl
wanting to be the icon.
In college, he remembers
studying late with a new leaf
moon for a history exam on
Indians and the Early Settlers
of the 1800s.
Pocahontas was an Indian guide
(but he can't remember from
which tribe). He remembers
that women guides were
often called sleeping dictionaries,
exotic women translating words
and finding less treacherous routes
full of gold nuggets or beaver
pelts for fur trappers,
explorers, white men . . . . These men,
most of the time, slept
with their guides, maybe
like "Lewis and Clark." Lewis
remembers that his Clark
is waiting for him—overwhelmed
and starved at the table rubbing
his hard abs, still trying
to figure out which road to take:
K-town to San Diego,
interstate or road?
The Disney Girl's mother
pulls her away from him,
thinking her daughter is bothering
him or maybe she knows about
Lewis and Clark.

She apologizes in broken English,
different from his *Chicaga* accent.
The sunset is different in this
land without the best architecture
like the Wrigley or the John Hancock
buildings rising taller than the natural
red earth skyscrapers and clouds.
Different without the one lonely
Water Tower he feels kinship with
because it survived the Great Fire.
Lewis wonders all this, in the dying
light of day, as he orders
from another Pocahontas in a
maroon uniform, in Kayenta,
Arizona, on the Navajo Reservation
without the barbed wired fences,
sanctioned by a White government
after the Long Walk—
the forced walk of thousands
of Navajos in the same coldsnap
of a Chicago winter, unforgiving.
Lewis sees the tiny exploitations again,
seemingly harmless toys given
to countless Navajo girls, and knows
they too must walk the Long Walk—
without a map, they walk from
Ft. Defiance to Bosque Redondo
which is their same journey
through life, the corn pollen path
over the reservation and past
every modern man-made city.

After all this,
It's like imagining
how old, how big
the universe is—
endless,
endless . . . .

Starlight, galaxies, silent
comets. Red maple leaves
spiraling up to the sky
like another great fire swallowing
Chicago under a blinding sandstorm.
In 1864, the Long Walk begins
in cold ice; in 1871 the Great Chicago
Fire ends in white flames . . . .
Clark still tracing his fingernail
along Route 66 to nowhere.
Children figure-eight skating
on ice, circling and circling Chicago.
The empty eyes of the Code Talkers
watching the Japanese war
prisoners, who were kept in war
camps on the reservation and
locked in photograph on the opposite
side of the wall, black and white stills.
Clark dancing shirtless under strobe—
he's slick as a black crow's feathers.
Four cows still resting under
a gas station's awning—

But all joining in a single thought,
a moment blowing away in Kayenta's
coming monsoon or on
the sunny beaches of San Diego.

Lewis clears his voice:

"I'll have four
Whoppers with cheese and
no onions . . . ."

My Feminist Grandmother

Grandma didn't have to march on
Washington, D.C., or resist
Politicians. Bras, she did not
Own. Feminism does not exist.

Grandma owns all the land, cows, corn.
Her words are final; we listen.
Arguments end. And the word
Feminism does not exist.

Our clans are passed through our mothers.
What's his clan? Always make sure he's
Different. Grandma will always know.
Feminism does not exist.

Her daughters never move from home—
Grandma can arrange marriages
And bargains for her son-in-law.

However, a male in-law may
Never look upon Grandmother's
Beautiful face—know this is very taboo.

Our creator, Changing Woman,
Made all that there is: Earth,
Squash blossoms, sheep, stars, life, men . . . .
Feminism does not exist.

Divorce is rare, when it happens—
Her sons will protect their sister.
Put all his belongings outside.

I tell Grandma of Eve, dark veils,
Patriarchy. I go on to say
Many women have no voice, can
Be beaten, and wait on their men.

Grandma, did you know you have to
Take on Grandpa's name? *Quit telling
Jokes like Coyote.*

But, she does love my tales
Of Amazons, warrior women.
She replies, *they're just like Navajos.*

Man Living on the Rock

Alone. Non-existent. Ephemeral.

I am empty like my closest family, the Sun, the Moon, the Stars, the Meteors . . . . Every day I watch them rise and fall, rise and fall. I am frozen on a desolate rock ringing through the cosmos like a blind bird flying at night amid blinking fireflies.

I have a block body, a bit too symmetrical and perfect. I have a hole etched through my round head, barely thin enough to hold a thought. My Creator scraped away my knowing. I would never know another warm soul. How does "warm to the touch" feel?

I pray for rain sometimes, so I can watch the cornstalks grow from season to season and feel the coolest raindrops fall on my body's outline. When a sudden breeze blows the rain off me, they are only sad hints. I've heard of coffee and hints of cinnamon and mints added to it, like shapes in the fog, maybe shapes in mist.

Shhhh . . . listen and look for the tiger's breath.
                    A Vietnamese monk once said to me.
            He knew me as something real and holy.

I don't remember my birth, and immortality is not me. Time on this rock is a tornado's sweep, cruel and unforgiving. There is no love, like there is no end. Time is where the sky and earth meet. Where they meet in a forest. An oak tree in the forest where a leaf is being chewed by a little deer. The deer's eyelid and the glassy vision, which is round.

                                    Time is round.

I meet many people each sunrise. They touch me and smile sometimes; sometimes they wonder about me like they would some petrified dinosaur egg. They really never see me; they leave without ever touching the loneliness. I once overheard two Navajos from a nearby reservation sitting in their red truck talking. One talked about a beautiful dark-eyed Navajo girl he'd met at a '49 the night before.

"Did you ask about her clans?"

"Nope, just fun," said the lucky one with a sly grin.

I thought to be young and alive and to feel flesh would be like a drop of water touching my thirsty lips. Sex for me is only chalk dust, not the creamy marshmallow feeling they laughed about.

I eavesdropped for a few more minutes before they left without ever noticing me listening to them. But the one sly Navajo did say something I'll never forget.

"Don't ever waste a wish."

I made a wish.

I wished for love, for purpose, and I wished a vandal
would chisel me off this Earth. Because that for me is death,
or because that for me is life, my wish.

So tell me how a man should live.

Here I am, next to you:
A petroglyph on rock.

Coyote's *Ad Infinitum*

E Pluribus Unum

On the beach, under a big red umbrella, Coyote finishes reading

About King Midas and his touch. But greed became Midas's curse:

He could never bathe in cold river water, never eat cherries,

Never love. Coyote wouldn't make that same mistake

As he claps his hands.

One Coyote standing by the sea, a multitude of seagulls circling

Overhead, and then there are two smiling Coyotes.

A great story and a great idea, Brother.

Two Coyotes standing by the sea as a sailboat lazily drifts by.

Four Coyotes standing by the sea clap their hands.

Sadly, with his power, Midas turned his daughter into a golden statue.

16 smiling Coyotes appear by the sea: imagine stepping

Into a carnival's house of mirrors:

A perfect reflection all around . . . *ad infinitum* . . . .

Dolphins gather at the surf to watch.

A thunder-clap pierces the salt air,

144 Coyotes clapping an ovation by the sea . . . . All Midas

Wanted was to hug his daughter. Coyote upon Coyote

Multiply stories upon stories, multiply idea upon idea:

One takes the gift of fire back and hands everyone magic wands.

One blows out all the stars like candles.

One turns all men into women and all women into men.

Now there are more men in the world than women.

One wipes out poverty, pestilence, war and orchids—

Coyote loses himself over and over again.

Which one of his selves is the original?

She was so happy to see him. She ran and hugged her father, Midas.

One gives all animals speech; the dolphins and seagulls

Begin arguing. One makes everyone into brown-skinned people.

Everyone becomes "Indian." Coyote tries to find himself,

Just as Midas tried to bite into an apple, a lost wish.

Just remember Coyote is there, *to infinity,*

Changing everything from oak leaves to tide lines

To butterfly cocoons. Sometimes, when a sock, a $5 dollar bill,

Or a small engine plane goes missing,

It's just Coyote trying to remember. One expands the earth

To the size of Jupiter, so man, animals,

Gods, plants can live together. In Paris,

A Monet beachscape shows 16 coyotes frolicking

In the sands of *La Saille*. Coyote under his beach umbrella

Picks up his next book, *Cinderella,* and reads, *Once upon a time . . . .*

A '49 Love Chant

after an Egyptian poet,
thirty-five centuries ago

The color of corn she planted today
Prepares to speak—the sound of a fire
Cooking sweet corn, sweeter than honey.
Her love awaits me on the river's shore.
The Female River flows between us
As the Slicing Reed Clan awaits warm blood.

The new corn is ripe to pick. Each ear, blood
Coral with leaves as green as jasper. Today
I have decided that the love between us
Is stronger than the deadly reeds that fire
Passions. My hope is to walk on her shore,
To kiss her, hold her, and taste her honey-

Bread made of corn, water, petals, honey,
And best of all, her love for me. Our blood
Carries the same message of oneness. Her shore
Is time; the sand—our union of today,
Tomorrow, and yesterday. She is Fire
Wolf and I sit thinking how to bring us

Together. The green reeds separate us.
They want to taste blood more than bees' honey.
The reeds are quicker than thunder and fire
Does not burn them. I know they wait for blood—
To take my red life, then my love. Today
With the setting sun, I will swim to her shore.

I swallow turquoise for courage. The shore
Is lit by moonlight and the reeds keep us
Apart no more. I sang a song today
For Spider Woman about love and honey
Bees working. As I swim, I can feel blood-
Thirsty reeds brushing me, slicing hot like fire.

Shijéí, love, it is love that gives me fire
And strength. It is love that lulls the dark shore
Reeds to sleep. My heart slices through fast blood
Currents, the moon guides me. Hope helps us
To be one song as I taste her honey-
Sweet lips. She will whisper her song today,

Thank you, giving Spider Woman. Our fire
Will burn brightly on the river's sandy shore.
I have lived. Still the reeds await my blood.

A Postcard from Van Gogh

Small brushing strokes—
The feel of oil on the back,
Rubbing hands.

A good cooked meal—
Heavy cream sauce with pasta.
Garlic bread, warm.

We're out by the pool
Imagining a tranquil river.

The sound of water falls
With pineapples growing all around me.

Stars heavy as snowflakes
Reflect off the surface
As I begin my Coyote story
(I always tell this story, it seems romantic).

Coyote puts his hand in the pouch,
Pulling out a singing ember of burning
Turquoise. He tries to place it in the sky
Expertly like a surgeon or a card house
Builder. But, like all of us, frustration

And quick schemes . . . .

Two weeks later—

I pick out the postcard from my mailbox:

The J. Paul Getty Museum, Los Angeles
(It reads in small print on back)

Vincent Van Gogh's "Irises"
(Oil on canvas, 71 x 93 cm)

Purple splashes of paint; thick full petals
Ready to fall. Green leaves, rich enough
For cows to eat. Irises are almost as pretty
As orchids. One iris I notice stands out deep

And cold as ivory or snow . . . .

Coyote picks up the bag of stars—
All singing and whispering and blinking—
Bright as marigolds and shakes the bag
Like shaking out a blanket—hard and quick—

In perfect script the postcard ends:

I miss you
Love,

Above us the stars are singing.

Storm Patterns

after the Tuba City stylized Navajo rug

Black   Black   Black   Black   Clouds   Edges

Clouds   Black   Edges   Beauty   Red   Edges

Spiderwoman   Underground   Weaves   Together   Edges

Loom   Weft   Wool   Lazy-lines   First   Woman

Stumbles   Into   Her   Home   Webs   Edges

Wefts   Looms   Black   Sky   Above   Rain

First   Drops   Fall   Black   Spirit   Edges

Ants   Run   More   More   Dark   Lines

Spinning   Wool   Into   Clouds   Rain   Thunder

Enter   Her   Home   Learn   Weaving   Edges

Center

Lightning   Black   Clouds   West   Wind   Edges

East   Mountain   North   Thunder   South   Edges

Mountain   Red   Wind   White   Thunder   Strike

Water   Earth   First   Woman   Learns   Edges

Wool   Dyeing   Black   Red   White   Mixing

Edges   Waterbugs   Sing   Spiderwoman   Teaches   Edges

Falling   Arrows   Falling   Feathers   Falling   Clouds

Ending   Winter   Calling   Spring   Thunder   Edges

Four   Lightning   Bolts   Strike   Center   Edges

Navajos   Learn   Black   Edges   Black   Black

43

 **More Coyote Stories . . .**

The Dark World

Ałk' idídą́ą́' jiní

                                        Listen and remember.
The wind blows from all directions.
Look at the skin on your fingertips. Can you see the trails
                                        The wind left?
When we were created, the wind blew.
It is the wind that comes out of our mouths.
                                                It gives us life.
Grandma Spider Woman's voice drifted off . . .
                                        The wind took her story—

Sitting alone in neither day nor night,
        I am called *Áłtsé Hastiin,* First Man.
Sitting alone in neither despair nor hope,
        I am part being, part nothing, part man, part alive.

Outside someone escaped his dark world.
        He ran with awkward steps away from the officer's heels
Which sounded like dull spurs. With slurred speech, he yelled,
        "It was magic that set me free! Magic! Magic!"
The sound of breaking beer bottles also ran after him
        With the night wind, who whispered this story to me.

In the far reaches of my mind, Thought Woman appeared.
        She spoke and I thought . . .
I wonder if the cop caught that wino.
        She spoke and I thought . . .
I hope he didn't; I don't need no company tonight.

This cell   which has no people or furry animals
It is the First World again.
This cell   which has no sun, moon or stars
It is the Black World again.

First Woman lives here   She is trying to build a fire
                                        Made of turquoise and coral logs
                                        To guide me home.

But I can't see any fires to lead me back.

Earlier, I saw a star made of cheap brass.
          It shone bright from the captured lightning
In the ceiling. Tamed and broken like a painted war pony,
          The lights buzzed with a soft purr.
                              The star
Was pinned to Dan Begay's pressed blue uniform.
          The tribal officer walked the barred halls
Where he inspected other drunks and some wife-beaters
          In the Navajo Tribe's Tuba City jail.

Then he commanded the cells to become the First World:

     "Lights Out!"

The Mist People live here   I can't see their bodies made
                                   Of singing water in this dark.

The lights went out as fast as lightning could run.

Dan Begay's voice was like Spider Woman's own power of creation.
She wove storm rugs together with long strands
Made of time, dark clouds, rain, mud, thunder.

When each rug was done, it was as beautiful as
The storm's last drops summoning the Rainbow Priest's blessings.
But it meant that someone was complete.
So we die.

The cornfields yellow.
Someone's grandfather falls into a deep sleep.
The wind ceases to blow.
An elk steps onto the Interstate.

And it all becomes dark again.

The Insect People live here   I can feel her sharp steps.
                                           A black widow climbs
                                           The length of my brown chest.

I touched the cold wall and tried to scratch my way through,
Into the next world, the Blue World, like Locust did.

Locust freed the holy beings from darkness by digging his way through
The different layers of sky, to the world where all birds exist.

Swallows, Crows, Macaws, Penguins, Turkeys . . . .

The tribal cop caught me driving a car in this glittering world,
Unknown to me, I was weaving the road like a swimming salmon.

I was drinking cold beer.
I didn't have a license.
I didn't know who I was.
I was drinking hot wine.
And the tribal cop sent me back to the Underworld.

Why did I do this?

As Áłtsé Hastiin, they didn't know who I was.
They forgot where they came from; they forgot their language.
Now I sit with the taste of urine, vomit and whiskey mints.

After each story told, Grandma Spider Woman
Always warned me to never forget: Remember and know—
She said a person without story isn't a person at all.
He is lost.

Dead men and dead women.

Coyote lives here somewhere   Out there in the night, his tracks
                                     Lead away from many quarrels.

After the beings emerged from the First World,
Coyote threw a rock into a deep lake.
The beings watched it sink with a splash,
And each ripple shook the beings' anger.

The people were mad because of Coyote's words:
          "If the rock floats, people live forever.
          If the rock sinks, people will die . . . ."

Gambling a Good Night Away

The Vegas sky, bright
Lights, no stars, no moon,
Just an artificial biology:
A source of darkness.
Airplanes fly over a new
Sin, a city of money,
Like dragonflies.
The ground sprouts skyscrapers,
Cobalt bingo halls, tourists
And mouse traps. No longer
Does the ground give turnips,
Tobacco leaves or cocoa.
I just turned a $20
Into nothing, into a sharp
Shark's tooth cutting
My skin . . . . Like the old
Navajo woman who gambled,
Gambled and gambled
Her own two children away.
Thinking they were her last
Two wooly sheep hiding
In the empty corral. We both
Lost quicker than I can say
"A Quarter-pounder with extra
Cheese." With no more money
In my pockets, I sit down
To eat a salad and a turkey
Sandwich, something
I charged. However, as I order,
My gambling buddy, Hoof Man,

Interrupts. His tired voice adds:
No mayo, no mayo. People put
Mayo on everything. I once
Ordered asparagus and they
Put mayo on it. He sobs through
Dinner. At 3 a.m., I notice
An older Mexican, no, Indian
Woman circling a slot machine,
Looking for someone,
Or for a hidden quarter.
It should be time for the quiet,
The weight of a star,
The green dollar,
To put us to sleep.
But the woman still looks
At twilight for her night children.
At the edge of the city,
Coyote laughs, amassing all
The wealth of corn, coins
And children. The emptiness
Of a dollar puts us to sleep
With hope,
And some think maybe
Love will play a part.
Good night Monster of Night,
Vegas. Good night. Good night
Coyote, Angel of Luck.

A Strong Male Rain

The air dances with wet sand off golden dunes.
The horse begins to get excited
From the whispers of rolling thunder in the distance.
A tidal wave of dust swallows the sky.
A heavy rainstorm is coming.

Slowly he crawls across the sky, angry.
He's large and bumpy with thick, strapping gray muscles.
This storm cloud is male, that's what Grandma says.
"When the clouds gather anger, they cry thunder and rain.
            This is the Male Rain."

The sudden winds kick up sand into my eyes. I blink.
In a drying puddle from yesterday's storm, I see Darcy's face.
Darcy, a Jewish girl from Phoenix—
A friend also afraid of the Male Rain.
Her brother Ean brought on her fears.

Grandma brought on mine.
She told us kids to sit still and don't talk during a storm
Or we'd get struck by lightning.
When Darcy was young, she used to sit at the window
And watch the lightning show during monsoon season.

Ean walked to his sister by the window.
He grinned his teen-age teeth and said,
"You know, if you stand too close to the window,
            A *Kugelblitz* will get you."
"A *Kugelblitz*?" she questioned.

"Yeah, a ball of lightning to chase you."
She never watched the light show again.
Instead during stormy nights, she silently cried in bed.
Little Jewish tears added to the monsoon's rain.
She told me this story one rainy night.

I told her about the Male Rain and what not to do during a storm.
She told me about Ean and his tale of the *Kugelblitz*.
I guess Jews and Navajos aren't all that different.
We were both afraid of thunderstorms.
We have other past storms we were afraid of too.
She had the Holocaust
And I had America.

Lightning flashes . . . . Thunder follows . . . .
I begin whipping my horse, trying to escape the storms.

Coyote Took Her Class

for my teacher, Beckian Fritz-Goldberg

Looking to the Southwest, there she was teaching a group of lizards.
Her black hair wavy like corn tassels. Her class is made up of lizards
who come from either Arizona or Wisconsin. Sometimes as far away as
New York or Russia or Antarctica, they come. She taught them tough
penmanship, table manners and ballroom dancing poems. The desert
cacti heard the night stories from Wind Boy. Overnight, the cacti fruits
blossomed into fiery jewels. She also taught her lizards how to write a
subversive textual poem. She taught them how to pull down the clouds.

If you expect it, then it isn't subversive: i.e. the interobang?! But always
remember one of her commandments:

> *To each his own, as long as he pays for my beer. A sign*
> *of a great writer.*

From the North, almost four years ago, at noon, I entered her class. We are
now more familiar perhaps. We have compatible immune systems. I am
still learning her like mapping

                                        the human heart.

Where are the bunny rabbits hiding or Eve massaging her one
        white wing?

I know there are too many cowboy boots in the world, where are
        all the good poems?

The other day she taught me math, "If Jane has 2 apples and John has

2 apples, and they run towards each other, who will turn to applesauce first?" She wrote limericks to pass Geometry (in H.S.). As a result, I got a point for each limerick in order to pass her math class. *Obscene angles of the isosceles triangles (her teacher gave her a "D," just so he would never have to see her again).*

Coyote + Silence = Death.

She comes from poetry and a small town in _____, _____, where
　　　it's always _____.

Part X . . . *Beckian speaks* [Coyote interjects]

　　I now live in a boring city, Phoenix. Old Nature poetry could never be written about it because it's too hot, it's hot, it's hot [she was born during a May snowstorm]. *I'd much rather write about old cities with a Golden Gate Bridge. I could never write a Phoenix poem. Driving to my house is boring, but there is a mad burning splash—a greenish-gold course—mixed with saguaros* [there are too many golf balls and men]. *However, one day, stuck on a wooden electrical pole or a tall saguaro somewhere is an ad written in black marker:*

CAT FURNITURE
Call (602) 123-4567

　　What the hell!? Are they selling couches made of cat fur or what? My cat uses the Oriental rug in the house (is that cat furniture?) as a scratching mat. My husband bought her a little oriental rug from Home Depot, so she wouldn't scratch the expensive one. It didn't work. But, the cat does like oriental-theme furniture. I just wanted to call the people, who sell cat furniture, to see what they're selling.

In her backyard, her cat Fuzz jumps a baby cottontail . . . .

With fur floating up into the air, I learned that there are some stupid people in the world. I don't like cats much (because I'm of the Coyote Clan, remember?). We wrote a poem today with the theme: the ass of the exquisite horse. It was like a turquoise horse chant. How joyous his neigh!

> *Begin it with an absurd premise like, old shoes*
> *running around . . . .*
>> *Spontaneous human combustion is cool.*

I like all those weird names for fish, because they have a lot of consonants and no vowels—

BARRACUDA.
> *A BRRCD is subversive.*
> [Navajos aren't supposed to eat fish. I heard because they're
>> related to the Snake Clan]

I like the inside of a froggy body and somersaulting children
> *off the side of a Swiss Mountain.*

> *Guilt.*
>> *I only felt guilty once because I once owned a*
> *bike and I let it rot.*

[Likewise, I once stole Water Monster's baby and she destroyed the Yellow World, looking/flooding.]

> *Remember back when they used to teach penmanship.*
>> *I used to like the smooth*
> *penmanship paper and cool pencils. It was so sensuous.*

> *The paper was like the first sex I had,*
> *pulpy and smooth.*

57

Sliding together like honey across the kitchen table.
I used to steal all I could.

[Like sliding down a hill on a boulder playing with the
fun desert lizards, until I fell underneath and was crushed.]

I was once hired to drive a forklift. Did I know how? Well I drove my
forklift through the house on the ground, in the front door and out the
back, you get the picture.
I was fired.

> *I was glad they fired me. Yay! Now I can collect unemployment.*

Asdzáán Nizhóní, I call her. I can understand her. That's why I took her
class. At semester's end, I learned the answer to the math question: If
applesauce ran into the tree, it would become Jane, John and Spot. That's
called molecular conversion. I passed on my stories of Beckian to the
crickets, the Lice People, Hunger and Old Age. Still her former pupil
Wind Boy whistles her praises through the Mud Canyons of Desire. They
all tell me that the Glittering World should have more people whose voice
can be thunderous. They say her anger is a beautiful emerald too.

Next semester, she is teaching the Erotic Image . . . .

Spider Woman's Children

Each day she cards wool,
Releasing wet lambs.

She sings her song slowly for her sheep,
    For her rug, for her hands, for the sun above and
        For her mother who taught her the words so long ago.

        House Made of Dawn
            Made of Evening Light
                Of Dark Cloud
                    Yellow Corn Pollen

Shimásání, Grandma's hogan sits alone
Near the lowly adobe bluffs.
Loneliness overtakes the desert lands
As the night crawls from the east.
Her heart hungers for companionship.

        She soaks wool in the dyes of Spider Woman,
        The weaver of creation, weaving together
        Brown, yellow, black, white and red—
        Shades of her soul-self, children and life.

She pulls spindled threads like silk,
Intertwining them through the web-loom,
And the summer desert storms are caught
Within the geometric pattern—
White clouds, black lightning and water beetles.

None of her twelve children return,
Only when money for a new car or bills
Asks them to. They come to take her hard
Work, her beauty. *In beauty it is finished.*
Thank you, Creator, for my heart and hands.

Without ears, they are like prairie dogs, *dłǫ́ǫ́'*. Bark!
Bark! They don't understand her anymore and cry
Their wants: "Grandma, nice rug, I need to buy school clothes."
Each has lost her teachings and tongue. Her mind wants to
Reach out: *Please, stay. Talk to me, sha'áłchíní.*

Rising from a dark world beyond the Rainbow's blessing,
Their bright white smiles are payment for robbing her,
And quickly they return to their burrows
Deep in cold cities: Los Angeles, Phoenix . . .

Into the night her weaving comb
    Locks her tears into the wefts of wool,
        The much needed rain in the storm-pattern rug.

    Each night she cards wool,
    Releasing wet lambs.

The Rottweiler

At dusk, Coyote spotted Locust near the freshly made mound of red earth. Coyote's voice cracked like melting ice over crushed leaves. "Grandpa Nalnishe buried his son today." Naalnishí in Navajo means "One who works" or, loosely translated, Grandpa Worker.

Locust chirped, "Who was his son?"

Nicona. It is wrong to talk about the dead because their spirits are moving on to the next world, and we don't want to trap them here by accidentally calling them back. Nicona. But Coyote started to tell his story with the rising night and the coming rainstorm.

Nicona. We all remember the story. Grandpa went to the distant purple canyons where different gods dwell in Anasazi ruins, some say the gods Poverty and Sleep (or even the infectious Lice People). Grandpa went looking for his two lost lambs. One was the night's spirit and the other was the cloud's edges. He never found them. They are probably still sleeping under yucca trees or just too poor to come home, or lice as big as cows ate them. But that's a different story . . . .

Instead, after the moon fell into the canyons, Grandpa came home with a big dark dog. As mysterious as the rolling fog, Nicona came from the mist following Grandpa's riding horse home. We asked Grandpa, "How did you come up with your mystery dog's name?" because it isn't Navajo like Yazzie or Begay. He told us of a wise man in China, Hastiin Lo Chen, whom he speaks to each night in his dreams. One night, the wise China man gave Grandpa a gift, a rottweiler, and Lo Chen said, "Your dog's name is Nicona." From then on, we thought Grandpa accidentally nibbled on locoweed. Many questions always remained about Nicona.

How does a big orange-and-black-furred dog end up on the Navajo reservation, four worlds removed from Beijing?

Nicona and Grandpa became one, like father and son, except when it came to food. They never ate in the same space. As Grandpa roasted mutton in the hogan, Nicona ate outside. It is wrong to eat in front of dogs or cats (even though they are considered family). Together, they loved to gather sheep and cows. Nicona wasn't like Grandpa's own grandchildren, who hated to herd sheep. They needed to be near each other, like the harvest moon follows the planting moon. Stars smoothing the pitch of night, chasing each other forever . . . .

One day, Nicona almost swallowed a horned toad (he swallowed everything else, like rabbits and crows) near our hogan. Grandpa yelled at Nicona, "You never eat family. Leave him alone!" The horned toads are sacred beings, our grandfathers too. Nicona backed away, which gave character to the orange fur above his eyes. On that day it look like big tears. Nicona never attempted to eat another family member again.

Coyote stopped his story to gently pat the wet earth of Nicona's mound. Locust played a sweet sad melody that night for all to hear and know.

In bed, I listened to a howling coyote and some crickets chirping through the night while remembering Nicona's passing. It was my first weekend home after three months in boarding school, where the food was bad and they showed Bruce Lee movies over and over. Before the sun set, we ate our first dinner without Nicona guarding the doorway. I still remember Grandpa's hands, stained red from digging dark clay, as he ate a piece of salted frybread. It was the only thing Grandpa ate; his cold mutton ribs were still on a foil-wrapped plate, waiting. In the darkness, I heard the labored breaths of Grandpa trying to sleep himself out of sadness.

Coyote said, "Hágoónee'," to Nicona and Locust. He headed toward the purple canyons to tell the news to Sleep and Poverty and maybe even the Lice People, if they promised not to eat him. Coughing and almost in tears (Coyote hated sad stories), Coyote muttered, "Sheesh, I'll never watch another Karate movie again, it's too painful."

On the ground, the moonlight outlined the tiny tracks of the horned toad leading away from the drying mound. The sound of rolling thunder broke Locust's song. Soon the air would be electric with rain falling over Grandpa's lands.

Refusing to Be Blessed

Pick up the smooth stone at your boot tip—
Quickly blow the dust off the edge.
This is for Sexton's mother who died March
1959. This is for Sexton's father who died

June 1959. This is for love born in September
1949. When Autumn came, it left the trees bare.
Leaves are but whisper ready to become snow.
No sign of a harvest, no corn. This is for Anne.

I breathe out carbon, breathe in carbon, in early
October 1971. The stones in the river's currents
Are polished. I was conceived in the empty
Winter. Little did I know when Coyote threw

His one stone into the perfect pool, it meant
One by one, we die just as amber mosquitoes.
For the Navajo people, Coyote threw the stone
Into the ocean for our survival. Across the ocean,

Past television screens—Marie, sweet Marie—
This is for Marie's voice and scrolling words:
Tumor in the back of the head. The black birds
Fill the sky as icy hail: *It Must Have Been Love.*

September 2002, I have lived another year.
I wish Sweden to keep her goddess of music.
Another new moon passes and I understand
The word *terminal*. This is for Coyote

And his ability to hide his life force. This again
Is for understanding Sexton today. This is for
My mother who will weave an AIDS quilt.
She'll use a loom and yarn and tears, this is for

Love and hoping that when the universe ends
We never hear the splash. We never hear th—

She Is Ready to Weave

for poor Leda

1.

> *By the dark webs, her nape caught in his bill,*
> *He holds her helpless breast upon his breast.*
> —William Butler Yeats

The great Swan thrashing about—

Coyote witnessed the confusion of empty white
Feathers lying on the ground. First there was a woman
Almost nude, one full breast touching his beak

Under him, ready.

He wanted her to moan from his thrusts.
He had heard of Indian women, smooth perfect stones
To break, to swallow, to nudge.

And then nothing.

The stunned Swan watched a spider crawl into the reeds.
His confusion stood still in the settling dust.
His fast pulse-beat died.

2.

Soon a woman with long black hair appears at the river.
Walking as sensuous as rising smoke.

It is Spider Woman. She is beauty above, all around,
All around. The green frogs and water beetles sing her welcome.

She kneels over to fill her pots with cold water—
Her arm lightly caresses her leg as long and wet as the river.

    3.
Sing with me the Enemy Way.

Sing like bears, one thousand growls tearing meat off bone.
Sing like ants, one thousand stings to burn the forest down.
Sing like horses, one thousand hooves barreling tornadoes.

The yellow sky melts to shadows.

The frogs and water beetles
        Chant the Enemy Way song.
The clouds swirl and swirl into smoke.
        Angry fire ants rumble mountains.

The blue sky fills with raven claws.

Sing with me the Enemy Way.

Sing like bees, one thousand wings buzzing thunder.
Sing like snakes, one thousand rattles cracking the moon in half.
Sing like bears, one thousand growls tearing meat off bone.

She pushes back into the power: hot blue zig zag light—

        A white fury engulfs her, blinds her,
        Knocks her to the hard wet mud. She feels her body
        Tremble, not from fear, but surprise.

Who would dare?
Something brushes her thighs, her back, her nape.

Was it feathers or a beak? She feels his raw power, honey.

She pushes back into the powerful thunder buck, always smiling,

Almost moaning . . .   she whispers,

4.
The spider spins a web, ropes the sun,
Blows a hole on the ground bigger
And bigger. It grows big enough
To swallow the moon. Inside is her loom,
Her basket full with yarn and her comb,

She is ready to weave.

5.
Coyote saw a bright star falling
From the Male Rain and water beetles' anger.
Coyote saw a white bird falling—

It had a curved skinny neck.
It had a different beak from all other birds.

It fell . . .

Near where the Male and Female River
Cross, meet, become one.

Curiosity took over Coyote's thirst.
"Hello, Brother, what's your name?"

6.

Toward nightfall, Swan asked an odd question—
"Brother, are there any women in this world?"

Coyote thought, wondered and then pointed
To the river flowing East to West, the Female River.

"No, Coyote, I mean a real woman, breasts and blood.
A woman who walks, talks, cooks, makes things with her hands."

"Oh, you must mean Spider Woman. She does all those things."
Without thinking, Coyote cleverly added—

"She'll be by soon to gather water in her pots."
Coyote hid among the tall reeds to see a swan story unfold.

7.

A bee storm   —a thousand wings buzzing.

A powerful web swallows like a sandstorm.
Bolts of jagged flint strikes try to tame Neptune's storm.
But it is not his body. It is not his story.

This woman   Spider Woman

Her body   is more than his equal.

The skies are not his to take, his hidden language.

Swift and blinding and brutal—wooly yarn
        Made of Red Sky.
        Yarn made of Black Coal.

She spindles yarn made of Yellow Starlight.

The Swan could not fly through warp and wefts.
The Male Rain funnels cold ice. It burns the earth.
He had never been touched before. The frogs
Jump happily. His feathers and skin
Tear against reeds slashing like broken glass.

    8.
One star glares in the smoky sky.
The weaving is done.

                    One final black wool strand
                    Snakes through the wefts tightly.
          The comb is laid to her side. Nothing is left.

Just some burnt pinions floating,
Falling like powder snow . . .

Over a hurt, whimpering dog.

Four Days, Four Nights

A whirlwind swirls and swirls across the lands.
It is that soft wind that blows from our mouth.
Imagine all the places you have walked:

A grocery store, a grave, Las Vegas, East
Germany, China, the beach, the bull fight.
A whirlwind swirls and swirls across the lands—

We breathe that wind. Whistling through empty ice caves,
It passes you; it blows across the Earth.
Imagine all the places you have walked:

Tuba City, a military base
In Guam, the cornfields. Even near Grandma's death,
A whirlwind swirls and swirls across her lands.

Where does the wind go when we die? Your past—
The wind retraces all of your footprints,
Imagining all the places you have walked.

A journey that took one hundred years will take
Four days and four nights to erase your steps.
A whirlwind swirls and swirls across the lands.
Imagine all the places you have ever walked . . . .

 **Theory of Light**

A Sheep Dog Laments

after a Navajo lullaby

"Náshdóí yéé bikee' diniih."

The white woolly head chews air,
Green cud. The still sheep dog's ears
Are caught changing into
Radar dishes left listening to the locusts
Chanting the Enemy Way, in the half moon,
To the corn pollen dusting the night.

"The Mountain Lion's paws hurt. Come help
        me, little sheep."

"Náshdóí yéé bikee' diniih."

A lonely lamb finds the hurting
Mountain Lion—yawning and crying on
A boulder. A falling star becomes an epitaph.
The sheep dog walks a few steps
Into the blowing wind trying to find
The lost lamb. Above, a star falls bright blue.

"The Mountain Lion's paws hurt. Come help
        me, little sheep."

"Náshdóí yéé bikee' diniih."

The sheep dog howls.

"The Mountain Lion's paws hurt. Come help
    me, little sheep."

Overhead, a jet shakes the hogan as my mom
Wonders where the missing sheep have gone.
She knows we have fine sheep dogs, three
Rough mutts. At first light, we'll take the pick-up
Over the sand dunes to the edge of the canyons
To listen for a dog's howl. A shoe-game song
Turned lullaby, my mom sings of a terrible cat
Luring lambs. My mom blows out the kerosene
Lamp, I smile to hear it again:

"Náshdóí yéé bikee' diniih."

Buffalo Head Nickel

    1.

The sandstone wash that cuts through the Navajo-
Hopi land dispute, rabbit brush, canyons,
Barbed wire, hot cornfields and our water pump
Built in 1892 are thirsty.   Sheep and cows
Walk through the wash to get a drink from the well—
An easy way through the land disputes and canyons.

Grandma and her many grandchildren pump water,
Pump water from a spring well, deep enough to fill metal tanks
For coffee, mutton stew, frybread and drinking.
      Along the wash on dry sand grains, the sun
Reflects off a piece of aluminum and like a magpie
Or the eye to red.   I pick it up.

It's a buffalo head nickel, shiny as an eaglet's first cry.

It's like finding a flint arrowhead. *I wonder how the wash got it?*

The soldiers leave nothing and burn down our dripping peach trees,
      Corn, fat watermelons. Kill our sheep, horses and cows—
Their skulls stare at me: Why?
      They are trying to take the Nalnishe family to Ft. Sumner again.
But the soldiers never find us in our canyons carved from
Red earth rain   red wind   and Spider Woman's webs.
The male clouds above spill sheet lightning and Monster Slayer
      Isn't in our canyons tonight to control the hard light.
Kit Carson and his army men move on to Canyon de Chelly,
      Away from Sand Springs, away from our burning hogan
           Toward the House Made of Robin's Egg Dawn, far far east . . . .

Carson crosses a red river wash . . . Gushing water—
His appaloosa almost buckles, almost drowns.
  His twenty men follow like baby rabbits.
Carson lights a cigarette after beating the torrents.
Before moving on, he pulls out a sparkling coin
From a leather medicine bag taken from a dead Navajo.   The coin
Splashes like a toad into the shouting water.
A coin for his Irish luck or to thank the water?

  2.

Navajos leave our family's Enemy Way Ceremony (some call it a Squaw
Dance), shadows slipping back toward the San Francisco peaks
  Or Tuba City or Winslow. Grandma and Grandpa worked hard
To keep stomachs warm
On sweet melons   hot frybread   salty mutton ribs.
Late last night, in the crow's sky,
  My cousin Amy sneaked off with a Todachini boy
From Bird Springs. I never liked him.
He was too much like Coyote. I know
He went to Luepp Boarding school with me. He was mean,
With a good hair cut and a cute smile the girls liked. He led Amy away
To a hidden mud wash. I tried to follow them, bring them back,
But the wash kept its secret except for the occasional giggles,
Deep horse breaths. The wash acted like a canyon's echo
  Melting in the air, a howl and crumbling sandstone.

Amy wore her brand new velvet dress that Grandma just made
For the ceremony.   When Grandma was cleaning Amy's
Pretty dress, she yelled out like there was a snake in the hogan.
  Grandma found Amy and whipped her with a horse bridle.
Her red welts swelled like ant mounds on her smooth skin.
  Good thing Grandma didn't find out about the Todachini boy too.
    Amy's dress was as rare as abalone or purple tiger orchids.

Grandma had used expensive coins as buttons. Three pure silver
Buttons missing, each a rare buffalo head nickel;
Each swallowed song gone.
Never trust a Todachini boy.
I told you they were like Coyote, no good.   *Button, Button . . . .*
I wonder what happened to your buttons.
Did the wash take them as payment or
Did Todachini rip them off with a kiss?

    3.

The clans had to leave. Navajo called them Ayání.
Big Eaters.   Buffaloes.   Ayání.
There used to be many of them chewing up new sweet grass hairs
       At the edges of our canyons or near the Hopi mesas.
Chewing on wild strawberries by the San Francisco peaks.
Chewing delicate morning glories deep in the Colorado forests.
They walked to Mexico, stopped for a drink
From the Rio Grande.   They walked and walked and chewed
On new grass sprouting from the stones of the Aztecs' gold
Cities. We took only a few of them. They ate for us:
Crow, Navajo, Nez Pierce, the Five Great Nations . . . .
We took only a few of them; they are a part of us, like our own eyes.
They walked in clans grazing from Canada to New York
To the Yucatan. They scaled the Grand Canyons
As the Anasazi etched their images with sunlight into rock.

One day, railroads and white men cut through
       Their clans like flash flood, cutting through earth like cracks.
Cracks have their own paths to take no matter if they shatter
       Stained glass or erode corn soil into the oceans.
One by one: Buffalo Bill Cody   President Andrew Jackson
Iron horses   Gold rushes   God and priests
Gunned them all down because "savages" depended on Big Eaters.

Each buffalo was killed for its tongue, its heart, its brown skin . . . .
A meeting was called. Every living clan member thought about how
       They could all survive.   Some said they would hide
                In White Man's Greed.
Some said they would try to survive as buffaloes.
Many of the buffaloes changed form and became new coins.
They lived as nickels. When the last buffalo dies,
Will all the coins come back to life?

Theory of Light

The sky is a blanket of stars covering all of us.
The night is folding darkness girl.
—Luci Tapahonso

OFF – ON

A switch
Illuminates Einstein's
Three pages of thoughts
Like a camera bulb flash-blink
Capturing silhouettes,
And ignites God
As pure

Energy.

Tiny flecks of waves
Speed across time, across
The night sky like a lovers' meteor shower,
Across the desert, over our
Hogan, across my
Cornea.

Christ's star: a supernova
Sings, burning bright for days like rays
From a candle enticing bats or wise men. Navajos saw
This too when the flames in the sky began.
It was Coyote placing his

Last star, a reminder known as Mą'ii bisǫ'.

Mass can become energy:
For a second faster than time,
In front of an old trading post, Einstein's
Soul becomes a frozen static charge, the sparks
Seen in an eye-dazzler rug. The photograph's colors
Show him wearing a warbonnet slick with feathers, pure and thick, thick
As an angel's wing. The outline of his teeth's bright
Magnitude reaches out across history as a laugh
Or a quasar. Smiles all around him, a group
From Moenkopi's cliffs.

The Hopi Corn Maidens are in woven rug dresses.

Their hair tightly wound,
Spiral galaxies on each side of their heads.
A sign of fertility. Einstein admires the green corn-
Fields and the maiden's pacifist and pure ways of grinding blue corn into
Fine meal, all day long, then into paper-thin piki
Bread. Untouched. *War can't ever be made*
From good food. His white
Mustache moves

And looks
Like a fish's
Skeleton.

Behind the trading post, unseen on
The dirt, in the umbra cover of the sun, is a Navajo man
Drunk, grasping an empty whisky bottle.

One Hopi grandmother knows Albert
Einstein as a famous man, rather than just another white
Tourist the other corn maidens see. As a mother of twelve, she shares
His vision. He knows something about a star's souls and
Its hopes and she thinks of the

Equinox tonight—"The Moon Kachina comes, big as a ripe watermelon."

Moonlight
Comes from the piece of white shell
First Woman placed in the sky one winter night.
Even Navajos knew then that the energy and mass of stones
Could power the whole sky. A long time ago,
First Man placed a piece of turquoise
In the sky; its small mass became
Our sun.

A burning, burning ball of hydrogen-helium.

It burns to grow corn, melons,
Beans, and squash. It burns to grow fusion
And nuclear reactors. The Navajos mined raw uranium
For the White man for years, with bare hands. They ate their
Cold frybread and greasy mutton salted with shiny tailings. The miners
Went home like bees covered in a thin pollen. Their sheep drank
From radiated mine wells. The grandmothers butchered
And roasted more mutton for their working men,
Hungry grandchildren. In Los
Alamos, a Zuni family

Grinds winter corn for tortillas
And watches the volcanic smoke rise thick on the horizon.

Deadly fumes hot from Nagasaki. They see the Hopi Butterfly Maidens
On Bikini Island; a drunk Navajo who, once a miner,
Is now dying from radiation

Poisoning. Coughing blood. Pain
In the joints. Losing vision. An eclipse. The sun's core
Is made from turquoise and the moon's mass is made from radiant
White shell lighting the metallic half-life in susurrations
Across the Navajo-Hopi reservations.

It all ends—

In one pyroclastic flower engulfing clouds and light.

The Blue World

It is the wind

> *That blows from our mouths.*

We breathe wind.

> *Where does it go*

When we die?

A whirlwind blows across the Earth.

Noon, almost four years ago
I awoke on rocky beach:
Laguna Beach, California, to be precise.

The hospital named me Eve.
Since I forgot who I was, they called my illness amnesia
But my Navajo friend, Irma Begay, calls me *Áłtsé Asdzáán,*
> First Woman.

Irma says I am Navajo because of my facial features.
She says I have clans, but I don't know them
And can never be whole. Because of my brown skin,
Long silky black hair,
And the sharpness of my cheeks,

I am *Áłtsé Asdzáán,* born from water.

In the sea, kelp held me,
Drowning. Their cilia hairs moved me
To the next world, the crest, the surface.

Four white seagulls flew overhead
As the sun dried my floating shoulder.
The seagulls circled me,
I watched them—

Four days,
Four nights.

Until the beach, the cool brown sand
Absorbed me. He had blue-green eyes,
The blond EMT who touched my face,
Searching for a pulse. He pulled off
Seaweed caught around my wrists
And the few seashells in my hair.

"She's alive," he declared.

But was I?

Everywhere or nowhere,
The wind follows.

You breathe.

I once saw bats as thick as clouds
Flying out of caves in Mexico . . . .

Irma was a nurse from Crownpoint, New Mexico.

She's a full-blooded Navajo born for
The Deer Spring People, related to
      The Red Towering House People,
The Black Streak Wood People,
      The Bitter Water People.

I am one, I am nothing.

I am *Áłtsé Asdzáán,* born from oceans and white shells.

In the Second World of our Emergence,
All the birds came alive with songs and feathers.

The Bluejay's song, above
The Eagle's forever cry, above
The Hummingbird's fuzzy form, above
The Turkey's roundness, above
The Peacock's rainbow breath, above
The Crow's starless night, above
The Swallow's nest home, above
The Wind, the Many Birds' domain above.

We emerged from the soils like corn does.
Áłtsé Hastiin was first,
      Then me, *Áłtsé Asdzáán,*
          The Mist People,
             The Insect People
And Coyote, Badger, Mountain Lion . . . .

One Holy Being
      Followed another,
            Each blinking
                    Into existence in the Blue World.
Coyote, Corn Boy, Corn Beetle Girl, Talking God, Thought Woman . . . .
We emerged from the dawn as the sun does.

The first beings that greeted us
Were the Swallow People.
Their skin was feathered.
Their mouths were beaks.

They breathed wind.
They spoke in song, sweet sharpness.
They saw we were strangers,
But we had legs and arms like them.

They took us into their homes,
Their nests, families.

When you see a whirlwind
Blow by, it is wrong to enter it,
Because you must not interfere
With another's journey.

Be respectful; let the wind
Swirl past you.
Smile and imagine.

I once saw penguins floating on icebergs
Near the Los Angeles darkness to the South . . . .

Alma jokes with me, saying
I can only have twelve children,
The proper number
Of children a Navajo should have.
No more, no less.

She goes on to say,
Hopefully, I will have a set of twin boys.
If I have twins, their holy names are
Monster Slayer and Born for Water.

The Hero Twins of the Navajo.

She laughs and laughs, imagining
Her goddess, *Áłtsé Asdzáán,* living
In Seattle, Washington, near the cold sea.
First Man would no doubt be white with blue-
Green eyes. Maybe a cowboy, a congressman

Or a movie star. I would live in an apartment
With southwestern décor, a TV and a goldfish.
I would go to night school to become a Tribal
Secretary and my baby boys would be raised
In a daycare drinking Pepsi. My lost ones,

My own Hero Twins
To help me find my way home.
To battle my monsters:
Taxes, the Lice People, Bills, Diets . . . .

Save me, my children, remember me.

Mąʼii, Coyote . . . .

It was Coyote who entered her home.
It was the Swallow Chief's wife,
Swallow Woman. He talked to her,
He sat next to her feathers, he touched her leg,
He touched her stomach, he entered her.
He was breathing;
She was breathing.

Breathing wind together.

All the Holy Beings were banished.

We could no longer live in the Blue World.
Eagle flew to the edge of the Sky and found a hole
       To the next place, the Yellow World
Where the Male and Female Rivers divide all.
Eagle flew through the layers of Sky.
       All the Holy Beings followed.
Coyote waved goodbye to Swallow Woman.

We left.

I once saw two roadrunners racing
Down Route 66 trying to catch the sunset . . . .

Four days,
Four nights.

The wind erases your steps
All the way back to your mouth.

Just calm quiet

        Not even a breeze
        To rustle a feather.

Irma recited the Blue World in English.
Somehow I knew my own name

When she called me Áłtsé Asdzáán,
Because of my golden skin and slanted eyelids.

The look only a Navajo could have.
A mirror sees only a Navajo staring back.

I am someone, I am Navajo.
I am one, I am nothing.
I can learn
Or I can forget.

Grandmother Moon

Tonight is the lunar eclipse.
Tonight the moon blooms.
Tonight my grandma is home.

The cornfield carpets the canyon's basin.
A Navajo field of colored corn,
Red, Yellow, Blue and White
Grandma Nalnishí whispers to the moon.
Her turquoise jewels reflect the dinner fire.
In the distance, the bells of the sheep ring.
Overhead, the moon begins to glow.
Tonight is the lunar eclipse.
Tonight the moon blossoms.
Tonight my grandma is home.
Every year, the Crow Fair brings her family back.
She holds her sleeping grandchild.
In the security of her camp,
Grandma Black Eagle sings for the moon
And the booming drumbeats create the rhythm.
The Little Bighorn River reflects the starlit sky.
Through the trees the moon begins to glow.
Tonight is the lunar eclipse.
Tonight the moon burns.
A Hopi village rests quietly on a mesa.
In a rectangular room, she whispers a prayer
As the candlelight Kachinas dance on the wall.
Grandma Honyumtewa prays for the moon,
And a lone Kachina points out the window.
On the rooftop, an owl hoots "Who?"
Out the window, the moon begins to glow.

Tonight is the lunar eclipse.

Tonight the moon bleeds.

Tonight my grandma is home.

Relocated to a house in Oklahoma,

She lost her Cherokee homeland.

In her rocking chair, a tear drips off her cheek.

Grandma Webb cries for the moon

While fanning herself with a beaded Eagle-feather fan.

The air is sick as a loud car passes by,

And over the buildings, the moon begins to glow.

Tonight is the lunar eclipse.

Tonight the moon beckons.

Tonight all my grandmas are home.

Tonight they all see Grandmother Moon.

Tonight the moon glows deep like blood.

Tonight the moon is Indian.

Canyons Echo Grandma

for my voices

I remember those winter nights Grandma
Would tell me stories about Coyote.
He would try to trick the lizards,
Or rabbit, or try to steal lightning
From Father Sun's home beyond the canyons
To the East. The wind carries through corn

Stalks the sound of our voices singing corn
Songs for the harvest. We pick as Grandma's
Voice comes back in echo from her canyons.
Tonight the full moon stirs one lone coyote
Howling an answer, and above, lightning
Bugs glitter the August sky. A lizard

Hopes a moth will flutter to his forked lizard
Tongue. Hungry and tired from picking corn,
We fill the truck full of green ears lightning-
Fast, as the sweet smells coming from Grandma's
Fire roasting mutton quickens the coyotes'
Sharp barks for her cooking. The canyons

Magnify their barks whining; the canyons
Seem alive with night voices: owls, lizards
That silence sharp crickets, more coyotes
Joining in chant, someone shucking ripe corn,
Grandpa coughing, children pitching screams, Grandma
Trying to quiet them. Finally with lightning's

Shatter, she scolds them. "We don't run in lightning
Storms and we don't yell at night—the canyons
Can hear you. Their echoes," explains Grandma,
"Can conjure up the bad spirits. Lizard
Monsters and skinwalkers could be in the corn-
Fields. Be quiet, and don't be like Coyote."

The children are silent with fear—Coyote
Stories always do that. My fear of lightning
Comes from those old stories. I smile. The corn
Harvest is done and I know these canyons
Are alive with my voices: from lizards
Running across the clay desert to Grandma

Kneading tortilla dough. I know Coyote
Is out there in the darkness, like lightning
Waiting to strike, hoping to steal our corn.

In Between

Out of the little breath of oblivion
That is night
Take just
One star.
—Langston Hughes

1. Secrets

There is a waiting
Like the pages between a book,
Or a doorway,
Perhaps the moment when ice
Becomes water or
Water steam.

Only clouds know the secret

Floating above, space.

Above sunrise and sunset,

There is a perfect alignment, a border.
It could be noon or the one black bird
Flying through.

It could be the calm of an ocean, lapping sea coral,
Or the edge of sub-zero, smooth icy tanzanite.

Again the moon-egg illuminates the purity of bluejays.
Crickets sing the endless changing of light and hope.

Only clouds know the secret
Floating above.

2. Waiting (a Holy Being speaks)

The soft breeze drifts the story of crickets—
See and hear the words: *I stand in a world below. A blue*
Secret above. I wait to escape as other beings rise through
The space. Locust went first, the first to pierce the sky.
Locust faced four birds of destruction. He was so little
But powerful as a star. I wait to pass through the sky.

Grandmother below will help. Grandfather above waits.

Someone will give me a hand and pull me from in between.

Here below there is no snow, no earth,
Just dizziness and exclusion, as the dark water
Rises—angry bees, angry smoke—
Ready to sting, drown, erase.

3. Grapes

Creation is a mirror.
Turquoise Boy,
Moth Girl helped save
Cricket from the waters.

Just past a warm evening,
Before a pious night,
On a dandelion's back,
Deep in a forest by a great
Lake is the reflection.

Crickets sing as stars appear,
One by one, growing full and plump
As grapes. Sweet cool grapes,
Enough to fill a basket.

Ripe enough to stain clouds,
And the sky with a path . . . . Stars
Are everywhere in a blank universe.

Creation is a mirror—

Just take a look.

Written after "Knight Rise 2001," a permanent light/space installation, of the *James Turrell: Infinite Light* display, for the Scottsdale Museum of Contemporary Art.

Acknowledgments

Some poems previously appeared, often in earlier versions, with grateful acknowledgement in the following publications:
Expedition, Flyway: A Literary Review, Journal of Navajo Education, Hayden's Ferry Review, The Southern Anthology, Wicazo Sa Review, O Taste and See: Food Poems, Family Matters: Poems of our Families, Coyote Brings Fire, Arizona Highways.

The Scottsdale Museum of Contemporary Art commissioned the poem "In Between".

My deepest thanks to Beckian Fritz-Goldberg, G. Lynn Nelson, Laura Tohe, Norman Dubie, Alberto Rios, Jeannine Savard, Melissa Pritchard, Coyote, and The Deer Spring People, for their outstanding teachings and continuous revisions. Thank you for sharing your stories, songs and inspiration, without which this book would not have been possible, Roddy Yellowman, Scott Manning Stevens, Darcy Lazar, Forrest Ashby, Eddie Webb, John Nesbit, Tom and Susie Worker, Cee and Mary John, Sonny and Mary Black Eagle. Ahéhee' Jennifer Wheeler and Lizzie McNeil for your careful eye. Thanks to Patti Hartmann and the University of Arizona Press for hearing my voice. Furthermore, I am grateful to the generous support of the Patricia Roberts Harris Fellowship and the Navajo Nation Scholarship program.

Source Credits

Excerpt from "Leda and the Swan" reprinted with permission of Scribner, an imprint of Simon & Schuster Adult Published Group, from *The Collected Works of W.B. Yeats, Volume I: The Poems*, Revised. Edited by Richard J. Finneran. Copyright © 1928 by The Macmillan Company; copyright renewed © 1956 by Georgie Yeats. All rights reserved.

Excerpt from "A Song for the Direction of North" from *Blue Horses Rush In: Poems and Stories* by Luci Taphahonso. Copyright © 1997 Luci Tapahonso. Reprinted by permission of the University of Arizona Press.

Excerpt from "Stars" from *The Collected Poems of Langston Hughes* by Langston Hughes. Copyright © 1994 by the Estate of Langston Hughes. Used by permission of Alfred A. Knopf, a division of Random House, Inc.

Excerpt from "The Truth the Dead Know" from *All My Pretty Ones* by Anne Sexton. Copyright © 1962 by Anne Sexton, renewed 1990 by Linda G. Sexton. Reprinted by permission of Houghton Mifflin Company. All rights reserved.

About the Author

Hershman R. John was born in Torrance, California, and he was born Diné to the Deer Spring People. He grew up on the Navajo Reservation in Sand Springs, Arizona. He received his BA in English and his MFA in Poetry at Arizona State University. Some honors include an award in poetry from *The Southern Anthology* (1999), a Patricia Roberts Harris Fellowship (1995–98), a poem—*Roadrunner Fragment #17*—dedicated in bronze for a public arts display in Tempe, Arizona (2002), and a NEH Summer Institute Fellowship (2003). The Scottsdale Museum of Contemporary Art has commissioned his poetry for two different art exhibits. His work has appeared in anthologies and journals, such as *Flyway: A Literary Review, Hayden's Ferry Review, Journal of Navajo Education, O Taste and See: Food Poems, Puerto del Sol, Wicazo Sa Review . . . .* He is a residential faculty member at Phoenix College (MCCCD). In his spare time, he enjoys reading comic books, traveling to beaches, and eating out.